POEMS FOR HUSBANDS AND OTHER UNDERDOGS

BY

Michael Irving Phillips

Copyright 1982
All rights reserved
ISBN 0-9610516-2-0
Michael Irving. Phillips

Poems for Husbands and Other Underdogs
ISBN 0-9610516-2-0
© Michael Phillips
Hotcalaloo Press (Formerly Treetop Press)

No part of this book may be reproduced without prior written permission by the author.

Contact Michael Irving Phillips at

hotcalaloo@yahoo.com

www.hotcalaloobooks.com

Table of Contents

Introduction 5
Part I FOR HUSBANDS 7
    A.   BEFORE MARRIAGE 8

The Love Bush 8
Love and Marriage 9
Sophisticated Lady 10
Metamorphosis 11
My Reward 11
    B. THE HONEYMOON 14
Don't Change 14
    C.   THE HONEYMOON'S OVER 16
The Imposter 16
Peace of Mind 19
What Happened 19
Oral Sex 20
My Defiance 22
Hugs and Kisses 24
Why 26
Beau Does Not Dance Anymore 27
Shining The Bricks 29
My Reply 30
To Divorced Girls Who Have Reconsidered "Suicide" When The Rainbow Was Too Much 32

Part II FOR OTHER UNDERDOGS 35

The New Jews 36
I Am Not The Enemy 37
Jamaica Exile 42
I Wanted to Live   or   Drive-by Shooting 44
I Killed A Rat Today 47
Hope Springs Eternal 49
Two Problems 50
The Message 51
Here Come The Eighties 52
I Remember Vietnam 54
Good News 55
The Voice That Never Came 65

Introduction

Within recent years there has been a deluge of feminist literature. Part I of this work is by no means a retaliation but simply an attempt to present a point of view, seemingly extinct, the husband's. From the writer's observation, many husbands share these experiences and hopefully this presentation might bring about revelation and better understanding, particularly to wives, ex-wives and potential wives. This is the writer's aim.

The "Other Underdogs" are all powerless. They range from the stereotyped-as-lazy government (State) employee to the homeless unwanted refugee to the elderly.

Also, In some poems, such as *"The Love Bush"*, and *"I Am Not The Enemy"*, the author has drawn from his Jamaican background.

In this new edition, more than thirty years later, unfortunately. not much has changed. There have been more Vietnams. In some instances it probably has gotten worse. The grievances of husbands are totally ignored or unheard, except for comedians. But, this is no laughing matter. Marriage is in trouble! Divorce is rampant! Listen up! If the husband's perspective is never considered, then marriage will continue to be the greatest cause of divorce.

Part I

FOR HUSBANDS

A. Before Marriage
B. The Honeymoon
C. The Honeymoon's Over

A. **BEFORE MARRIAGE**

The Love Bush

The love bush is a golden vine
That in Jamaica you will find
It has no leaves
And for support
Must grow on trees.
Along their trunk and leaves and branches
It winds it's golden thread
Like a warm embrace
A warm embrace of love.
The Love Bush is a pretty sight
But it really is a parasite.

Visualize
A golden vine
Intertwined
With the leaves of green
A beautiful picture to be seen
The Love Bush is a pretty sight
But it really is a parasite.

And so did love envelop me
With its golden string
The sky was blue
The sun was bright
All was filled with such delight
1 could even hear angels sing
The Love Bush is a pretty sight
But it reul1y is a parasite.

But the sky was not blue
The sun was not bright
All was not filled with such delight
Angels singing -- lets be serious
How 1 must have been delirious
How could 1 have been so blind?
The parasite had fed upon my mind.
The Love Bush is a beautiful sight
But remember, please remember
It really is a parasite.

Love and Marriage

1 love you dear, you know it's true
I'd really like to live with you
But marry I will never do
For experts agree after much discourse
Marriage is the greatest cause of divorce.

I agree with you that love and marriage
Go together like a horse and carriage
But look through this window
What do you see
Choking the streets of our fair city?
Horseless carriages going to and fro.
The horse and carriage have had their day
And marriage too should be put away.

Sophisticated Lady

Sophisticated lady
Gathering friends to inflate your ego
Dumping friends
Those who held you dear
To polish up your image
Callously
Sophisticated lady
Narcissistic lady
All roads lead to you
Or else

Sophisticated lady
Narcissistic lady
You are not alone
But surrounded by other three dollar bills
But I still remember when
You had a heart
You could enjoy simple things
Were compassionate
Old time values meant something to you
And ulterior motivation did not
But now you are successful
A successful sophisticated lady
A successful sophisticated narcissistic lady
For your image shines brightly
It shines so bright
It hurts my eyes
It shines so bright
But it has no warmth
It makes me cold

It leaves you cold
It does not illuminate the darkness

Metamorphosis

I was just a larva
A lowly grub
Mired in my cocoon of drab existence.
Then you came by
Suddenly I could fly so high
I thought I'd become a butterfly
But when my love you did not return
Chafing from third degree burn
I realized I was just a moth
You are the flame, pretty but hot.
I know the danger
But I don't give a hoot
Here comes the moth again
But in an asbestos suit.

My Reward

What is happening to me?
My mind, my soul,
My whole body
Emotions, senses
Cease this mutiny!
Be strong; resist!

Have you forgot

The pain, the suffering
 That it had wrought?
You are no naive innocent
No siren song can capture you
You're battle hardened through and through
Besides you're too sophisticated too.
I love her
Stop! Remember your resolution
I love her
Be aloof, don't get involved
I love her
Limit yourself to mere flirtation
I love her
You'll be exposed, so vulnerable
I love her
Oh what a complete capitulation!

Thank you dear, you made me see
That love is not my enemy
All the songs and poetry
Of love
That in the past
Seemed so silly
Is now reality
To me.
All the fear, all the doubt
My love for you
Has wiped them out.
You have opened up my mind
To a happiness I sought
But never thought
I'd really ever find
You arouse in me

Such ecstasy
A euphoria with such intensity
You bring me pleasure
You bring me joy
For you, my starapple I'll never cloy.
It's not just your versatility
But most of all
You give to me
Appreciation
A sense of dignity.
Looking back life seemed so hard
Thank you God for this reward
Ahead, my love, my course is clear
Even though obstacles
Stand in the way
To make you happy
Till my dying day
My debt of happiness to
I will thus repay

B. **THE HONEYMOON**

Don't Change

I know that time
Will try
To disfigure you physically
But to me
You will be
Always beautiful
As that July night We first met.
Time does make distortions
Relentlessly
But he is not omnipotent
Your destiny is in your own hands
And so I beg you
As the years pass
Don't change
Don't change the way you look at me
With adoring emerald eyes
That lighten up my soul
Don't change your sensitivity
To all my cares, my hopes, my fears
Don't change your tolerance
Of my weaknesses
And expect infallibility of me.
Don't change the way we disagree
Without rancor nor hostility
But with respect for each other's individuality

Above all
Don't change the love you've shown to me
I'm addicted to it hopelessly
My love for you knows no boundary
And so these pleas that I make to you
Are also pledges I myself will do
So that, together
We will age but not grow stale
We will age but not grow tedious
We will age but not grow old
But be forever young.

C. **THE HONEYMOON'S OVER**

The Imposter

Honey, you know I have to go play tennis,
The other three depend on me
And I do have the next hour free
I know you work as hard as me
Wash the clothes
Clean the house
Feed the kids
Buy the weekly groceries
And so on

Honey, all my tasks are done
I'd love to talk, but I gotta run
I'll be back in time for our dinner date
But this weekly game just cannot wait
I know you work as hard as me
Wash the clothes
Clean the house
Feed the kids
Buy the weekly groceries
And so on

Dear, in your estimation
All I do is recreation
I share all those chores with you
Come on give me some credit too
I know you work as hard as me
Wash the clothes

Clean the house
Feed the kids
Buy the daily groceries
And so on

To go to tennis he had no chance
His wife had piped, to her tune he'd dance
But it was not always this way
There was a time he had more say
And she was so very meek and mild
A fragile thing, so warm and docile
Anything he did, she would agree
How did she change to such degree?
From Polyanna to Simon Legree
Full of storm and criticism
Complaints, dissatisfaction and derision
To blow his nose, he needs permission
But, how did this change come about?
He searches through his memory
To find the answer is not easy
For it happened so gradually.
Hie remembered way back when
By her smile, he would give in
If she pouted, to her wishes he'd bow
He told himself it was unimportant anyhow
As the years passed, he would about just
Let her opinions prevail to avoid a fuss.
So the problem, he himself created
Now she's strong, he -- emasculated.

Dear, my elbow just does not feel right
I think I'll skip tennis tonight

Besides, you probably need me
To help you cut the celery.
I know you work harder than me
Wash the clothes
Clean the house
Feed the kids
Buy the daily groceries
And so on

Husbands do not look down on him
Because he is at the mercy of his spouse's whim
Look at yourself and you might discover
Great transformations since you were her lover
Do you still back pack or play a sport?
Do you still roam caves or sail your boat?
Your next golf date do you tell or seek permission?
If thirty minutes late, do you feel contrition?
Think back very carefully
And ask, "Was that decision really made by me?"
And wives, don't overreact to such criticism
For if you fall in such a system
Your own happiness would be a victim.
So search your soul and heart and mind
"Am I the same person, or did I leave her behind"?

Peace of Mind

Giving me a piece of your mind every day
Is keeping my peace of mind far away
Besides you can't spare it
It's too narrow to share it
And you have lost most of it anyway

What Happened

What happened in the church that day
When family and friends did hear us say
At God's altar with knees bent low
We each did make a sacred vow
I - to love and honour you
You - to love, honour and obey
But since that day
I have no say
I must love, honour and obey
And obey, and obey
Just because you've become my wife
You don't have to boss my life
I loved you then for your mind
Not just for your cute behind
But since you've no longer been a miss
Your idea of wedded bliss
Is to deprive me of my mind
To follow yours meekly behind
Just because you've become my wife
You don't have to dominate my life
That symbol of love, that wedding band
That I slipped on your finger with trembling hand

Instead of treating it like a jewel
You use it on me as a tool
Despite my protest and my groan
To chip away at my backbone
Just because you've become my wife
You don't have to domineer my life
No, let us relive those days
When we'd compete in seeking ways
To please, to show we cared
Oh those precious moments we shared
If prodigals can be born again
Why can't we be wed again?

Oral Sex

I just could not believe my ears
Despite being married all these years
Your wife wants only oral sex!
Oral sex!
You lucky man
You"re one in a million
Do you understand ?
Husbands, husbands everywhere
Sexually starved, in deep despair
And your wife of many a year
Desires oral sex
Then is there hope
That my wife might be next? Fat chance I
Slim chance

No chance
Funny thing before we were wed
We spent such great times in bed
She was full of passion and fire
Ten years later, bed's just a place to retire
For she has got an aching head
It occurs 'often as she touches the bed
Or I'm accused of ruining her mood
For failing to put away left-over food
A trifle - I think so -
Especially when it was done
Two weeks ago.
How I had such high hopes
Not knowing that Kinsey and those experts
Were playing us husbands for dopes
Each year I waited
For her sex drive to peak
But instead of stronger
It only got weak.
Maybe I've become a lousy lover
So I followed the "Joy Of Sex"
From cover to cover
No significant difference did it make
Perhaps a pretty outside opinion
I need to take
And oral sex is your wife's thing
Despite twelve years of wearing your wedding ring
....
But why such a doleful countenance
You should be happy;
Sing! Shout! Dance!
Or are you such a prude
You think it's crude?

Don't be blue
Now nice girls do.
"*You don't understand*", he said
"*My wife*", and then he sadly shook his head
"*Is no different from the rest
Sex - twice a month at best
Any more
She puts up such a squawk.
Her beloved oral sex
Is really a bore
And means nothing more
Than a subject on which
She loves only to talk.*"

My Defiance

Her warm body
lying beside me
cold
now cold to my touch
a touch which once
with just my little finger
would send her passions
flying
and desires for me
burning and
yearning
for me
for me!

but now the years
have neutralized my touch
so that even
the stroking of my tongue
the caressing of my fingers
all over,
across, between, within
bring no response
and learn instead
to accept rejection
but the blazing desires
within me
the rigidity which
wont go down
as my defiance grows
and hardens
it's a rebellion
within me
but thoughts
of you
dreams, yes fantasies
of you
transformed into reality
that alone
can free me from
this agony

Hugs and Kisses

I'm frustrated
I'm so vexed
Hugs and kisses
But no sex

Conversations,
You're so witty
After all these years
And still so pretty
But your beauty
Is strictly ornamental
While my sex drive
Is pretty fundamental
Just not ready
For celibacy

I'm frustrated
I'm so vexed
Hugs and kisses
But no sex

You desire me no more
That is very clear
I should be understanding
But what should I do, my dear
When my throbbing cock is standing?
I'm horny all the time
Blame it on this nursery rhyme
*"I love little pussy,
Her coat is so warm ...."*

Please don't think my morals loose
It's all because of Mother Goose

I'm frustrated
I'm so vexed
Hugs and kisses
But no sex

So help me Rhonda
Be a friend
Help me have good sex again
And for this I promise you
That you will have a great time too
So have sex with me
Passions stored will overflow
And we will share such ecstasy
"Oh yes! Oh yes!" she said
I leaped for joy
And flew amongst the clouds with glee
You see
Her "yes" was just my fantasy

In reality
"You should be ashamed", she said
"Don't bother me
I don't care much for such ecstasy
I'll tell you why
I have bigger fish to fry
Unless you divorce your mate
With me you'll never have a date
In the meantime
Learn to masturbate."
Gulp!

Why

I was only trying to please you
But you served me my teeth
For lunch
I was only trying to please you
I failed
Bear it like a man.
You were trying to hurt me
You succeeded.
Congratulations

My fragmented spirits
Unlike Humpty Dumpty
Have been put together again
With hope and optimism
But are more fragile
So please tell me why
Should I
Continue to try ?

Beau Does Not Dance Anymore

And Beau does not dance anymore
It was a rapturous dance
It was a dance of anticipation
Of his daily walk
Yes, my Beaujangles was a dog of grace
A walk! A walk! A walk! A walk!
He danced
Up on his two hind legs
This large black poodle
Eyes shining with excitement
Mouth open
Tongue out
Front feet pawing the air almost rhythmically
Moving them to right
To left
With little two-footed leaps
Sideways also
But opposite
To right, to left
It was a spontaneous dance
No piper to pay
No command to obey
It was a dance of exhilaration
But, Beau
Does not dance anymore

Then Carly came
So dainty and innocent
She looked
But full of rough play

And boundless energy
They played together
They slept together
The ate together
Out of the very same dish
They were inseparable
Such an understanding
Such a close relationship
But, she would not let him dance
No, she would not let him dance

She would charge his dancing feet
With barks and flashing teeth
"Let me be" he seemed to say
But she would continue relentlessly
'Til Beau could scarcely stand
On four legs
Much less dance on two.

Mind you
They get on splendidly
Beau seems happy
No empty space
She's filled his life
But, Beau
Does not dance anymore

And you too my dear
Have filled my life
But, like Beau
I do not dance anymore

Shining The Bricks

I must continue to shine the bricks
They are so dull
And red
And even though I think
No
I know
These bricks were not designed
For shine
But still
I must continue to shine the bricks

So while others are out
Drinking in noisy smoke filled bars
Listening to loud but rhythmic music
Under the mistaken notion
That they are having fun
And play
At home
I stay
Shining the bricks.
But one day
Friends will visit
And they'll say
"How did you ever get bricks
To shine that way?"
I'll just shrug
But with pride.
So until that day
I"ll just shine away
While you never seem to cease

To laugh and play
But
Your bricks will never be
A conversation piece
Your bricks will never be
As shine
As mine.

My Reply

You know it seems to me
You are always ostracizing me
Everything I do, in your eye
Is wrong, but consider this reply
Be fore I do
Let me point out to you
In plays today
It is OK
For the characters to say
The filthiest word
You've ever heard
But only if it fits the part
Adds realism to the art
But it can't
If frivolous or irrelevant.

I remember vividly
How it was a shock
When new to this country
Fresh off the dock

I heard a lady
Considered quite a wit
Exclaim quite routinely
The epithet "shit".
Now I know, in this society
There was no impropriety
Everyone uses such words with impunity
Except me, maybe
I stuck fast to attitudes past
Even facing torrents of abuse
Dam and hell are the worst I use.
You yourself know, I hate profanity
Although you used it often times on me
And I would just boil inwardly.
Before my reply I had to set the stage
To show the abyss of my rage
Though the preface is long
The reply- quite a switch
Just three short words
"*Fuck you bitch!*"

To Divorced Girls Who Have Reconsidered "Suicide" When The Rainbow Was Too Much

I love him still
There is no doubt
Although it's more than a year
Since I walked out
All those things he did to me
Made me crave my liberty
I could not stand the misery
For a whole year now, I've been free

Boy, how he used to infuriate
Me by his refusal to communicate
Did not support my aspirations
But instead he made it seem
Silly, unreal, a mere pipe dream
So by the marriage I felt bound
Trapped, confined, tied up, held down
Rut he was kind in his own way
And ns a provider he was O.K.
He never once forgot my birthday
Yes, he was kind,
I have got to say
As a lover he could not be beat
Made my body pulsate from head to feet
Rut T saw a new awakening
A brave new world outside was beckoning
I could at last be me
No longer just a prodigy
Of him, by being just his wife

I would start instead a brand new life
No more would he take me for granted
No more would I be so discontented
No more would I faithfully wait
For him to come home hours late
I'd find someone more considerate
I am told I still have charm and grace
A shapely figure, a pretty face
And that handsome guy at 2463
Was always complimenting me

I remember when I broke the news
He looked at me all confused
I knew then I had hurt him bad
"Serves him right" I thought. I was so glad
Vainly he tried to discourage me
I thought he would fall to his knee
Right upon his dignity
"Oh how sweet the taste of victory"
Since then I've been on many a date
Met guys with whom I can relate
Really truly communicate
But almost everytime I'd find
They were not interested in my mind
With divorced girls their goal was sex
And once achieved, moved to the next
And so I had to change my course
Finding no love, settled for intercourse
And how about my aspirations?
Drowning in my perspiration!

Of course I would not admit this publicly
But seem cheerful and full of glee

"How great this single life can be"
I wish there was some way
I could go back to him and say
"Please take me back, forgive this fool
I know 1 was wrong, so mean and cruel".
But pride prevents, and by this time
Someone else occupies his mind
It was my fault, I must confess
But I still Will give him hell at D.F.S.*

```
*Discussion for singles - singles discussion
group
```

Part II

FOR OTHER UNDERDOGS

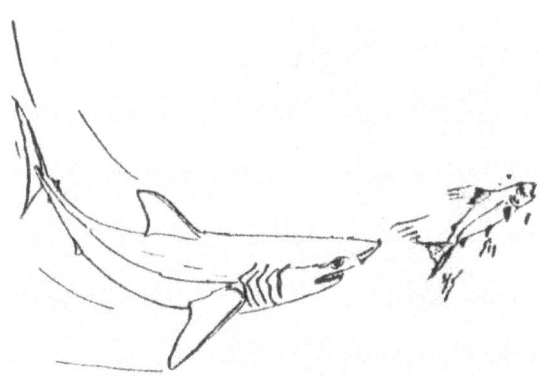

The New Jews

I am black
So I do not have to wear the star
For identification
Muslims now can be tracked
By compulsory registration
Mexicans will wear the smear
Of a rapist reputation
Millions will live in fear
Of their immediate deportation
For our new leader
Has body-slammed the constitution

For the Klan
There is jubilation
For once again
We'll become
A blue-eyed nation
"A black president!
What a disgrace!
Now those niggers
Will know their place".

What's this talk of diversity?
In our democracy
Hate is a great strategy
To create political popularity
Hate the blacks
Hate the Muslims
Hate Latinos too
Whether undocumented

Or legit as me and you

For we are the new Jews
Scapegoats of the nation
Lock them in the gas chambers
Of discrimination
And when the police
Shoot us down
They'll need no justification
Just routine persecution

So new Jew
Justice for all
Except you
Let me make it clear
You better learn to live in fear
For America elected a new leader
To the new Jews
He is the brand new
Adolph Hitler

I Am Not The Enemy

I am mad
That I must leave
I am sad that I must leave
But I must leave
There is no choice
But there is regret

There is no choice
But there is despair
There is no choice
But there is disillusionment
There is no choice
But there is righteous indignation
That I must leave
Is this all that I can take?
Packed in this solitary suitcase
This represents my years of sweat!
All my years
But I will not trade my blood
For my sweat
Still I must leave so much behind
To start over anew ....
But so much behind
That solitary suitcase is small
But I smuggle out on me
Valuable precious memories
Of
Khaki pants, both long and short
White blouse and blue middy skirt
Asham, stretcher, snowball
And back-and-front the best of all
Gieater cakes - two for a quattie
For lunch, cocoa bread and pattie
And the games we schoolchildren played
Hopscotch, chevy-chase, lemonade
Football with a tennis ball
Cricket with a "madman" ball
"Bowl-fe-bat" with a coconut frond
Schooldays with you sure was fun
But the teachers were so stern

They spared not the rod
They had the wrath of God
And you had really better learn

We grew up together
Although you are much older than me
And have a much longer history
But we did
I remember when you were just a colony
Like some beautiful woman, they admired you
Like some beautiful woman, they even worshipped you
But only for your beauty
Only superficially
They were not interested in your feelings
Your hopes
Your aspirations
Only theirs
Like some beautiful woman, they lusted after you
Like some beautiful woman, they exploited you
I witnessed your struggle
I was struggling too
But never against you

We both struggled through
Flood, hurricane and drought
Earthquake
Fire
Political dishonesty, rivalry and incompetency
Of both
JLP
And PNP
And lack of opportunity
For so many

But now Jamaica, you turn on me
But I am not the enemy
I know our masses were used
But not by me
I know our masses were abused
But not by me
I know they were treated unjustly
But not by me
I know they were exploited
But not by me
I did not bury my talent in the ground
Although I knew you were austere
All my possessions, I earned fairly
By hard untiring work
I served my fellow man well
But now so many turn on me
But I am not the enemy
I who understand their plight
Who understand their impatience
I understand their urgency
Their hostility
But, understand me
"I am not your enemy"

I am innocent
But my blood will not
Be on your hands
I'll spare you that
I'll start over again
In some foreign land
But I am mad
That I must leave
I am sad

That I must leave
For there is no remedy
But I'll never be the enemy

Jamaica Exile

Imprisoned in my home sweet home
Behind iron bars
That lets in the sunshine
But keeps out crime
Is not for me,
Anymore

For Jamaica bleeds
Stabbed in the heart repeatedly
By ruthless thugs of crime
And Jamaicans die
And fear death
Even behind their iron bars
That let in sunshine
But keeps out crime

And because of these
Ruthless thugs of crime
Jamaicans leave
Exiled to a foreign land
To leave behind
Distrusted politicians
Trapped in stereotypes
To serve a cynical public
And hopelessly watch
As crime plan after new crime plan
Fails
And even innocent children die
And heartless thugs triumph

To leave behind their
Yam and sweet potato
For foreign fast cholesterol-filled food
Leave behind their tropic nights
Filled with reggae music
Leave behind their seas so blue
Before it runs red
With the blood of Jamaica
Before laughter turns to screams
Before laughter turns to slaughter

To leave all that behind
For exile
In some uncaring foreign land
For anonymity
To adopt a foreign culture
And live in the memory
Of a crime-free Jamaica
Without iron bars
To let in sunshine
And to keep out crime
It is not a life
Without Jamaica
I am alive
But I am not kicking

**I Wanted to Live
 or
Drive-by Shooting**

I wanted to live
I wanted to run and jump
To laugh, to play
To dance, to sing
Even to cry some more
I wanted to live
Some more
More than six
Six short years
I wanted to live

Up three floors
Behind locked, bolted
And barricaded doors
On that lime green chair
With the gray shiny tape
On one tattered arm
But on which I liked to play
It searched me out
It found me there
I no longer will play
On that broken chair
I wanted to live
But your bullet found me there
I wanted to live
More than six
Six short years
I wanted to live

I wanted to live
I wanted to grow some more
I wanted to go to junior high
To senior high
Be a cheerleader
"Hey! Hey! Wha'd'ya say
Turn that ball the other way"
My graduation ceremony
My mother so proud of me
I wanted to live

I wanted to live
I wanted to love
To know the feeling
That first kiss
The exhilaration
To hunger for that special touch
Of that special one
And give myself to him
To wed
My little daughter
Just like me
But to work to make her
Better than me
I wanted to live

I wanted to live
I wanted to hold
My grandchildren in my lap
And tell them stories
Like my grandma

Used to do
And indulge them
Give them candies
Spoil them
Teach them to say
"Hello"
"How do you do?"
About the five little piggies
Who went to market.
Like my grandma
Used to do
I wanted to live
For more than six
Six short years
I wanted to live
I wanted to live

And how about you?
Do you feel remorse
Or am I just another notch
On your gun
Another boast to your buddies?
An uneventful incident?
Nothing?
Was it an armed robbery?
Or drug bust gone awry?
Or did you miss the head
Of some disrespectful friend?
And found 6-year old me
Instead?
Or was it just frivolity?
Could it have been
Deliberately?

Or just shooting
Your beloved gun
Indiscriminately?
But,
I wanted to live

I wanted to live
And the outrage of my death dies down
And my killer they tell me
Was abused from infancy
The system's to blame
Not he
It's because it stole his dignity
He was just trying to be a man
I should forgive
I should understand
But, I can not
Probably because
I wanted to live
I wanted to live
I wanted to live
And also because
I am dead

I Killed A Rat Today

I killed a rat today
No whimsical mouse
More timid than me
Rut a bona fide cat-challenging rat
Oh how long he stole from me

Oh how long he menaced me
Oh how long he taunted me
Took advantage of my age, my infirmity.
Imprisoned in my room
By that cruel warden, fear, With no one to care
I do not need a boy scout
To help me cross the street
Just give me safety
From the vibrant virile youth
That steal from me
That menace me
That taunt me
Because of my age, my infirmity.
What's happened
'Twas not long ago
When I was young
It was not so
The old we treated with respect
With dignity.
But I killed a rat today
Even though
'Twas a lucky blow
That laid him low.
My room cell window
Lets in light and noise
Allows me a view not worth viewing
"Black is beautiful" uglies the wall below
Already ugly
Old discarded people have no race
We're all Eskimos, yes Eskimos
Adrift, adrift on our ice floes
In the teeming stinking city.
But amidst the litter

Amidst trash cans yawning up their garbage
Out of that broken sidewalk
My eyes home in down there on an alien
Alien to this decaying city terrain
A flower,
Growing there?
Surviving there?
In that hostile environment
Hostile to it
Hostile to beauty
Hostile to me
Because of my age, my infirmity.
But I killed a rat today
I'm giddy with power
To hell with fear
I'll go out and smell that flower.

Hope Springs Eternal

Things are in an awful state
If by some tragic fate
You are employed by the State
But do not be disconsolate
The tips I have will alleviate
Your spirits they will elevate
But heed these tips, don't vacillate
And your progress will eventuate
Forget a decent salary
Think about the security
If you really want to get ahead
Get a part-time job instead

And then you'll have no time to play
So, for leisure you'll not have to pay
Ignore the important for a trifle
New ideas learn to stifle
Remember if you work hard
More work will be your reward
Backstabbing is a useful tool
"Yes sir boss" is the golden rule
Non-State jobs, people grow and grow
But the longer here, the less you know
Boredom devastates your mind
Your paycheck falls so far behind
You're afraid to leave
You complain and grieve
The public look upon you like dirt
And just when you lose all self-worth
Reduced to a robot-going through the motion
Cheer up. you're now ready for promotion

Two Problems

Who is going to take me ?
A refugee
With no country Just a liability
I'd work for free Just to be free
Yes, I'll even welcome slavery
But even that brings enmity
From underpaid and unemployed.
My propaganda value is gone
No more use to anyone
Oh West! O East! give me a chance

Play any tune and I will dance!
No hope, no hope in sight
Oh Malthus, you were absolutely right
What is to be my fate?
Why was I born decades late?

Oh my dear what shall we do?
Our car's two years old
And we can't afford a new.

The Message

We've closed the door
Seek liberty here no more
Seek opportunity here no more
We do not have enough liberty to share
Anymore
We do not have enough opportunity to share
Anymore
Traditions disappear
Under the harsh glare of reality
We've lots right here like you
Seeking liberty and opportunity too
But we are locking the gates
Against them too
Gates that laid open so long
Their rusty hinges protested
But oiled with apathy, selfishness and insensitivity
"As long as it's not closed to ME "
We've closed the door
And quite easily.
So go back from whence you came

We've changed the rules
It's a brand new more exciting game
Tell all the world,
Every Harry, Dick and Tom
We've swapped human values
For the biggest bomb.

Here Come The Eighties

Hostages taken in Iran
By Time magazine's '79 man
Years ago we may have told some lies
Some of the hostages may indeed be spies
But we will never sympathize
With Terrorism - let me emphasize
Innocent victims
Do you realize their sufferings?
Sometimes blindfolded, sometimes bound
Bewildered, imprisoned, restricted, underfed, under-nourished, isolated, harassed, brainwashed, vilified, and humiliated
For no proven crime or scheme
But our allies have hesitated
For the sake of gasoline

Soviets invade Afghanistan
Send millions of dollars to Pakistan
Spare no expense
For her defense

Her vulnerability
Now our responsibility
As leader of the free
As lover of the free
So we will respond with tanks and guns and jets and
bombs and mines and rockets and all sorts of military
hardware   .
And we should -
Let me make it absolutely clear
But in Chicago today
Thousands of schoolteachers are without pay

Energy crises loom
Cassandras foretell shivering doom
Can technology
Save the economy
From increasing dependency
On OPEC and oil companies
Conspiracies?
Shall we
Burn sulphurous coals
And pollute the plain
With acid rain?
Or is the atom our salvation?
But can we avoid
Meltdown, cancer, radiation?
I am not timid nor picky nor ignorant of the tremendous
benefit the friendly atom could be to all creation .....
But   .
I'd hate for my grandson
To be a mutation.

I Remember Vietnam

Question: "At a bullfight, how do we tell an American?"
Answer: "He is the only one cheering for the bull".
The bull's destiny is to be killed for sport and entertainment. The bull has the cards stacked against it. The bull is the dog, so to speak, the underdog. The American cheers for the bull, because it cheers for fairness, compassion and justice. These are the qualities which have revered America throughout the world even more than her economic, scientific and military accomplishments. Throughout the world, we were the good guys. In Viet Nam at the bullfight we were the ones who tried to machine gun the bull.
Yes, I remember Viet Nam. Everyone wants to forget it. The memory of the holocaust of

Nazi Germany is kept alive, while Viet Nam is to be buried. We have to remember Viet Mam, even though it is a horrible stain on our history. But we must be vigilant lest it happens again. As it is said "he who forgets the past is doomed to relive it".
Yes, I remember Viet Nam. First we entered the Vietnamese civil war supposedly at the behest of the acknowledged corrupt government of South Vietnam. Shortly after we were there, their government was overthrown by the military. Our alleged objective was to prevent the spread of international communism, the red peril, the domino theory, to save them from the Vietnamese Communists, the
Chinese Communists, the Soviet Communists, etc.

Good News

We've come to liberate you Vietnamese
To lift you up from off your knees
To give you our justice, to right your wrong
Let's eliminate the Viet Cong
Let's eliminate the Viet Cong
Let's go!
Can't you hear what we said
But no one moved,
They all were dead.

Yes, I remember Viet Nam. Viet Nam has had a history of fighting off invaders. They fought off the Chinese, the Japanese the French, whose legacy was an artificial division of the country into North Vietnam and South Vietnam. The Geneva Treaty requiring elections and eventual re-unification was broken by the south when it seemed evident that the popular liberator, Ho Chi Minh, of the communist north would win. Civil war resulted. Enter the U.S.
We were advisors at first, who would only "shoot back if fired upon." Little did the undernourished, insignificant, Vietnamese barely able to eke out an existence know that they were to come up against the awesome power, technology and might of the American war machine. So Goliath took on David. President Lyndon Johnson reaped devastation on them. They withstood. President Nixon, promising a secret plan to end the war succeeded him. It soon became apparent his secret plan was to "bomb them back to the stone age" a popular expression of the time.

Red or Dead

B-52's, B-52's overhead
Vietnamese falling
Red, blood red, and dead

Many people did not realize the extent of the bombing of Viet Nam and surrounding areas. "Wee did not bomb them enough" is still common-place. Thankfully, there were no atom bombs. However there , were big bombs, medium sized bombs, little bombs, bomblets, laser bombs, acoustic bombs, napalm bombs, truck and anti-personnel mines.
There were the most sophisticated bombers, gunships, helicopters, supertankers, B-52's, fighter aircraft in the arsenal. By the end of 1971, the U.S. had dropped "on an area the size of Texas six million tons of bombs and other aerial munitions, three times the total tonnage used in World War II".

Vietnamese Woman

"Vietnamese woman, please stop awhile
Tell me please, where is your child
Don't run away, I am your friend
I've come thousands of miles, for you to defend
Was she Killed by a dirty commie?"
"No, she was killed by a B-52 bombie"

Indiscriminate killing of men, women and children by impersonal bombs was bad enough. But our brave fighting men often faced the dilemma of discerning friend from foe. In this way even unarmed women and children were killed face to face by our men. The horror of such killings in the Mylai massacre of an entire village by our soldiers was no isolated incident.

Nothing Personal

Half-starved Vietnamese boy
This is a gun, it's not a toy
I hate to shoot you in your bed
But you might really be a red.

Naked Vietnamese lad
Pulling the trigger makes me sad
I wish you had a uniform on
So I'd he sure you were a Viet Cong

Vietnamese boy so underfed
Maybe you will be better dead
Your house is burnt, your parents killed
With so much grief your heart is filled

Vietnamese kid, please, man to man
It's nothing personal, you understand
I have my orders to obey
I must do what President Nixon say.

Vietnamese boy, so dejected
President Nixon wants to be re-elected
And you'll die better with the knowledge
This brings him nearer the electoral college

President Nixon was re-elected by a landslide. The people had spoken decisively. They did not want the anti-war McGovern. It was just a game. "We're number one. We're number one". The unranked Vietnamese would not give up or give in! Our prestige as a world power was at stake. Right or wrong, sovereignty, compassion, independence, justice, fairness meant nothing. Anything other than victory was too embarrassing for number one. Winning was the only thing.

When

Nixon, Nixon, Tricky Dick
Kill the Vietnamese till we're sick
Bomb I Dismember! Mutilate!
Burn! Disfigure! Devastate!
Fathers, mothers, kids - they're all the same
This we do in freedoms name
And lose respect and pride and fame
For demagogues, disillusionment and shame
When will we all regain our head?
Not till all the Vietnamese are dead?

Where was the moral outcry? Where were the Right-to-Lifers, the Moral Majority, the Billy Grahams, the Churches, the Religious and Political leaders? Where were they? Busy "Sieg Heiling" President Nixon to greater devastation. That's where.
There were a few exceptions. I remember Senator Wayne Morse. I remember the Quakers. I remember Jane Fonda. (St. Jane

as I called her. Too bad she wasn't from Arkansas as she should be Jane of Ark). Many good citizens still would like to burn her at the stake. There were of course others. How can we forget the thousands of college students who took to the street in demonstration and confrontation. They were America's conscience. Their reward was abuse, derision, beatings. shootings, imprisonment, and even death. At least Germans claimed ignorance of the Nazis, but in the Vietnamese war, we knew. yes, we knew. It was piped in daily fresh from the front right to the air conditioned comfort of our living room via TV.

Excuse Me TV Addict

Mr. American in front of your TV
Switch off "Laugh In" and think of me
You say you are saving us from the VC
But your bombs are blind, they cannot see
I hate to interrupt you In prime time
But this is more important than "What's My Line"
I know you are taxed up to the hilt
But with this tax, our sons are kilt

I do not mean to impose on you
With the Orioles leading 3 to 2
But I am desperate, you would be too
If so much "help" was killing you

Your help's burnt our hut

Your help's ruined our land
Our fertile fields now productive as sand
You have murdered our son, even our daughter
Accidental you say - cop a plea of manslaughter
It's not that I am not grateful,
I am, I am
But I beg you, beseech you,
Please Uncle Sam
Help us no more and get out Viet Nam.

Eventually we did get out Vietnam. After a last ditch crescendo of bombing more widespread than before, Nixon ended the war ironically in the manner that McGovern said he would have. By this time more than 1.3 million Vietnamese (population then about 3.4 million) and more than 56,000 Americans had been killed at a cost of more than 141 billion dollars.
But the legacy continued. Johnny did not come marching home to hurrahs. The war had been lost. It seemed America transferred the guilt of an unpopular war to these veterans. Besides, the senseless killings had scarred so many of their minds, making readjustment very difficult. The prevalence of mental disorders and addiction among them resulted. Others are now suffering the latent effects of Agent Orange with which they had contaminated the Vietnamese fields and streams in order to defoliate the forests there. But the greatest legacy of all was that by such heinous crimes, our

sense of right and wrong became distorted at home. Looting, pillaging, senseless killing justified abroad found its way home. The "it's OK if you're successful or not caught" gained ascendancy and is still prevalent today. If our government could sell us that war, they could sell us anything.

I remember Vietnam. But the time is now. All over the world at this time, there is potential for more Vietnams. Powerful forces are promoting a policy of the support of vicious dictatorships against the will of their people. The same old rhetoric used in Viet Nam is being served up. It seems to me if colonial America was today struggling for independence from Britain, the present day Republic of the USA would brand out heroes communists, force them into the communist camp and join Britain against them. So, when they come to you and say "Let us go save the world from communism and keep America free for democracy by doing a better less costly job of demolishing another small underdeveloped country," Let us say "No! Hell no!" Why? Because, we remember Vietnam.

The machine gun is being loaded to shoot the bull. Let's cheer for the bull. Toro! Toro!

More Vietnams

Good News

We've come to liberate you Vietnamese
To lift you up from off your knees
To give you our justice, to right your wrong
Let's eliminate the Viet Cong!
Let's eliminate the Viet Cong!
Let's go!
 Can't you hear what we said?
But no one moved
They all were dead

Years later
More Good News

We've come to liberate you ~~Vietnamese~~ Iraqis
To lift you up from off your knees
To give you our justice, to right your wrong
Now just where are those WMD's?
Now just where are those WMD's?
Aw... does not matter a hill of beans
Though now your country lay in ruins
Don't be angry.
Don't get hot
In years to come you will thank me
For bringing you democracy
Whether you requested it, or not.
Let's go! Can't you hear what we said?
But no one moved
They all were dead

We've come to liberate you Afghanistanese
To lift you up from off your knees
To give you our justice, to right your wrong
Let's eliminate the Taliban!
Let's eliminate the Taliban!
Oft we kill both friend and foe
But it's not really carnage,
Chalk it up instead
To mere collateral damage.
Let's go! Can't you hear what we said?
But no one moved
They all were dead

Onward our Christian soldiers
Now into Muslim lands they go
Dealing death and destruction
For dragon teeth to sow
Enough! Enough!
This I beg you please
Break the cycle
Cease this brutal repetition
Let the countries choose
Their own destinies
So at last there'll be
Finally
No more good news

The Voice That Never Came

"Leave the brother alone
We all know where he's coming from
Just because he don't
Talk that jive
Nor drive
A Buick 225
Air conditioned with power windows
Like you Who
Talk militant
To awe your friends
Or to belittle this brother
Just because he don't
Sniff cocaine
Have your distinction
Of being schooled in jail
Just because he ...
And you know it too
... is someone that's hard to find
A black brother that's truly genuine."

But,
No such voice came
No such voice dared to come
Against the popular The new popular
"Lef the man alone
Him trouble you?
Just because him drive big car
While you don't
Just because him wear coat and tie
While you don't
Just because him have big job

Wid no callous pan him hand
No sweat pon him brow
No hole in him shoe
No beard pan him face
No rass clawth from him mouth
Uhnuh tink him is not one ah we.
Uhnuh wrong
Im is one ah we
I know him
Many of you
Know him too
But 'fraid fe speak
And claim uhnuh brave
But uhnuh too dam weak."

But,
No such voice came
No such voice dared to come
Against the popular
The new popular
The new "enlightened" popular
Newly freed from repression
To form a new repression
A dogma exchange.
Silence is not golden
It stinks.

Note: (Third verse is in Jamaican dialect.)

www.ingramcontent.com/pod-product-compliance
Lightning Source LLC
Chambersburg PA
CBHW072016060426
42446CB00043B/2564